cutest ever
TODDLER
KNITS

cutest ever
TODDLER
KNITS

OVER 20 ADORABLE PROJECTS TO KNIT

VAL PIERCE

TRAFALGAR SQUARE
North Pomfret, Vermont

First published in the United States of America in 2013 by
Trafalgar Square Books
North Pomfret, VT 05053

10 9 8 7 6 5 4 3 2 1

Copyright © 2013 in text: Val Pierce
Copyright © 2013 Photography New Holland Image Library

ISBN 978-1-57076-567-4

Library of Congress Control Number: 2012934270

Publisher: Lliane Clarke
Project Editor: Simona Hill
Designer: Tracy Loughlin
Photographer: Graham Gillies
Production Manager: Olga Dementiev
Printed and bound Toppan Leefung (China) Ltd

Contents

Introduction

Knitting is growing in popularity and there has been a resurgence of interest in this delightful craft. There is something very rewarding about creating a garment for someone special in your life and it's even more pleasing to see the garment being worn.

Manufacturer's now tempt us with desirable collections of fashionable and thoroughly wearable patterns and mouthwatering selections of softly textured yarns. In fact, the range of yarns available is mind-blowing with new textures, finishes, and eco-friendly products being added to collections all the time. The colors are stunning, ranging from the most delicate pastels to vibrant bright tones, making the choice you have when deciding which yarn to use for a project an absolute pleasure.

Having already designed projects for tiny babies in my previous book I have now created a special collection of projects to fit toddlers. These pretty and practical designs for girls and boys will keep them warm and cozy while they play. There are also some extra-special projects for days out ranging from a gorgeous Scandinavian outfit with matching bobble hat and a shawl-collared sweater. For fashion-conscious little girls there's a soft lacy hat with matching fingerless gloves and a braided hairband complete with bow.

As well as clothes there are some very cute play toys including a fabulous fish and a sweet play bag complete with smiley-faced fruit.

All the patterns are rated according to level of difficulty and range from beginner right through to the more experienced knitter.

I have added tips and a techniques section, so whatever your skill level and experience there will be a project suitable.

Happy Knitting!

Materials and Accessories

YARNS

It can be quite intimidating for a new knitter to decide which yarns to use for a project. All the projects in the book have specified yarns but you can substitute these for different yarns. Just make sure you keep to the same ply or weight recommended in the pattern and knit a gauge swatch to check that your choice of yarn will turn out to the same dimensions as the one specified. Increase your needle size if your gauge is tight. Decrease your needle size if your gauge is loose. If you decide to change yarns then it is possible that your garment will look different than the one in this book.

ACCESSORIES

A few basic tools are essential for knitters. Invest in some good-quality needles since these will give you many years of service. A tape measure, stitch holders, row markers, cable needle, a good quality sharp pair of needlework scissors and wool needles are recommended too. A knitting bag is also a very handy thing in which to store your work in progress; not only does it keep it clean while you are knitting, you can store the patterns and yarns you are using all in one place ready to begin work.

Techniques

CASTING ON AND BINDING OFF

Make sure that your cast on and bind off stitches remain elastic by either working them reasonably loosely or using a larger size needle than stated if you think you work very tightly. As a general rule most binding off is done with the right side of the work facing.

KNIT AND PURL STITCHES

To create any fabric when beginning to knit there are two knitting stitches that need to be mastered. The knit stitch forms a ridged fabric known as garter stitch and can be used for many projects. The second stitch needed is a purl stitch which, when teamed with the knit stitch, creates stockinette stitch; this fabric is smooth on the right side and ridged on the wrong side. These two stitches can be used to work many beautiful patterns and decorative stitches and are the basis for all knitting.

A seed stitch pattern is created by alternating 1 knit stitch and 1 purl stitch on every row. The purl stitch is worked over the knitted stitch on the subsequent row.

INCREASING AND DECREASING

When working on some projects it is necessary to shape the pieces as you work. In order to do this you will need to lose or gain stitches on the rows as you knit. This is done by either increasing the number of stitches (done by knitting twice into the same stitch), or decreasing (achieved by knitting two stitches together).

WORKING WITH TWO COLORS

A couple of the designs in the book use more than one color in a row. When working these it is advisable to use the stranding method whereby you carry the yarn not in use fairly loosely across the back of the work as you knit. The yarn can be tied into the work on every third of fourth stitch to keep it neat and elastic. Care must be taken not to pull yarn too tightly when doing this otherwise it will result in puckering of the fabric.

WORKING FROM A CHART

Charts are read from bottom to top and usually from right to left. The first stitch of a chart is the bottom one on the right. Placing a straight edge of some kind under each row will help you keep your place in the chart when working the design.

INTARSIA

This is another method of adding color to your work, and is for the more experienced knitter. The motif or patterning is usually written onto a chart for you to follow row by row and the yarns used are not taken across the back of the work as in stranding, but each individual area of color is knitted using a separate piece of yarn. Winding small lengths of color onto bobbins or small pieces of card helps to eliminate tangling when using different colors in the same row.

GAUGE

Gauge is very often overlooked and can have a detrimental effect to your finished garments. Always check your gauge before you begin working, changing needle sizes to obtain the stated stitch count if needed. Remember, if you get fewer stitches to the inch (centimeter) than stated your gauge is too loose and a smaller needle is required. If you get more stitches to the inch (centimeter) than stated your gauge is too tight and a larger needle will be required. When measuring your gauge don't stretch the work out to make it fit or vice versa; knit up one or two samples until you get it just right.

MEASUREMENTS AND MEASURING

Most of the garments within this book are designed so that there will be an allowance for comfortable fit. When measuring pieces of knitting while working on your project it is much easier and more reliable to count the number of rows you have knitted. Sleeves and side seams will all sew up and fit so much better if the rows are the same. Sewing in sleeves sometimes causes problems, but if you pin and ease the sleeve in place before stitching you should get a good result. Raglan sleeves are easier to stitch in since they lay flat when sewing.

MAKING TASSELS

Cut a piece of card to the required tassel length and wind yarn around it to the desired thickness. Thread a piece of yarn through the wound thread and tie to hold the threads together. This forms the top of the tassel and the yarn is used to attach the tassel to your project. Slide off the card. Take a longer length of thread and wind around the threads to form the neck of the tassel. Knot the ends, Cut the other side of the loops. .

MAKING POMPOMS

Cut two circles of cardboard the diameter of the required finished pompom plus ¼ in (6 mm) for trimming. Carefully cut out a round hole in the center, a quarter of the diameter of the finished pompom. Wind wool around the cardboard and until the center hole is full. Place the point of the pair of scissors between the two pieces of cardboard and cut around, keeping the scissors between the two circles of card all the time. Using a double strand of wool, wrap the threads between the two circles of cardboard, knot firmly, and take away cardboard. Trim to shape.

FINISHING

After completing your work you will need to sew the pieces together. Sewing the pieces together is sometimes difficult to novice knitters but if you work slowly and carefully you will find it is quite simple. Back stitch gives a neat little ridge on the inside of the work. You can also work from the front of the knitting, laying the pieces to be sewn up on a flat surface so that you can catch adjacent stitches together, one from each piece as you sew. This is tricky to begin with but once the technique is mastered it gives an almost invisible seam, and makes matching patterns and stripes a lot easier. Take care to stretch front bands slightly when sewing them on as this gives a firmer and more professional finish to cardigans. Most patterns give instructions on finishing a particular garment for you to follow.

Always read the ball band of the yarn you have used, since this will give you details about pressing and washing your garment.

PICKING UP STITCHES

It takes a lot of practice to perfect this technique but here are a few ideas to help. Work through the complete stitch, using both strands; lifting just one strand will result in a hole in your work. Always pick up the number of stitches recommended, and make sure they are even on both sides of the neck and front. Measure the length of fronts of cardigans, then divide the number of stitches you need to pick up into the length, that way you will end up with a neat, even button or buttonhole band that sits flat. Work through the same stitch all the way up the fronts and always start 1 stitch in from the edge.

STRANDING YARNS FOR FAIR ISLE

Some of the designs in this book need the yarn not in use to be stranded across the back of the work. The spare yarn is carried across the back of the fabric, tying it in every third or fourth stitch. It is very easy to pull the spare yarn too tightly which will pucker the work, or leave it too loose which results in large uneven stitches. Weaving in the yarns will give a more dense and solid appearance to the fabric.

CABLES

Cables create an attractive and raised effect to the work. They are very easy to work and just entail slipping the stated amount of stitches off the main needle onto a special short cable needle. This small needle is then either taken to the front or back of the work and left while another quantity of stitches are worked from the main needle. You then return to the stitches on the cable needle and work across them in the normal way.

ADDING EXTRA LENGTH

It is quite easy to add extra length to stockinette stitch designs just by knitting a few extra rows before the start of the armhole shaping. However, where patterns, and especially Fair Isle patterns, are used, then adding extra rows is quite difficult since it will throw off the pattern sequences in the designs. Adding extra length to sleeves works on the same principle. If there are stripes on a design then make sure that you end both the sleeve length and the side seam length on the same color and row of the stripe to maintain the continuity of the pattern.

ABBREVIATIONS

beg begin, beginning

dec decrease by working 2 stitches together

inc increase by working into front and back of stitch

foll following

k knit

p purl

k2tog knit 2 stitches together, decreasing a stitch

M1 make a stitch by picking up horizontal strand lying before next stitch and working into back of it

psso pass slipped stitch over

p2tog purl 2 stitches together, decreasing a stitch

rem remain(ing)

RS right side

skpo slip 1, knit 1, pass slipped st over

sl 1 slip 1

st(s) stitch(es)

ss seed stitch

St st stockinette stitch

tbl through back of loops

tog together

WS wrong side

yo yarn over

NEEDLES SIZE CONVERSIONS

US	UK	Metric (mm)
0	14	2 mm
1	13	2.25 mm
2	12	2.75 mm
3	10	3.25 mm
4	–	3.5 mm
5	9	3.75 mm
6	8	4 mm
7	7	4.5 mm
8	6	5 mm
9	5	5.5 mm
10	4	6 mm
10 ½	3	6.5 mm
11	1	8 mm

YARN CONVERSIONS

US	UK/Australia
lace weight	1 ply
baby	2 ply
fingering	3 ply
sport weight	4 ply
worsted weight	8 ply, double knit, dk
fisherman or medium	10 ply, Aran
bulky	12 ply, chunky

Sweetheart Sweater

Knit a pretty sweater for the little sweetheart in your life. This soft sweater has buttons at the back of the neck so it's easy to get over a child's head. The stitches used are very simple: the heart on the front is knitted using the Intarsia method, which requires you to use separate balls of yarn when working the motif instead of weaving the yarns across the back of the work.

✳✳ Intermediate

To fit 2–3 years old

MEASUREMENTS
Chest 24 in (61 cm);
length from back neck 14 in (37 cm);
sleeve length 8 in (20cm)

MATERIALS
◆ Sublime Baby Cashmere merino silk DK,
75% extra fine merino wool / 20% silk /
   5% cashmere (50g; 127 yd / 116 m)
◆ 1 x 50 g ball Rosy (RP), shade 126;
◆ 5 x 50 g balls Vanilla (V), shade 3
◆ 3 small flower buttons and matching thread

◆ Knitting needles size US 3, 5 and 6 (UK 8, 9 and 10 / 3.25, 3.75 and 4 mm)
◆ Stitch holders

GAUGE
22 sts x 28 rows st st measures 4 in (10 cm) square, when knitted using US 6 (UK 8 / 4 mm) knitting needles

SPECIAL ABBREVIATIONS
SS = Seed stitch (UK moss stitch)

FRONT

Using US 5 (UK 9 / 3.75 mm) and vanilla, cast on 67 sts.

Work 10 rows in SS (seed stitch).

Change to US 6 (UK 8 / 4 mm).

Row 1: (RS) SS10, knit to last 10 sts, SS10.

Row 2: SS10, purl to last 10 sts, SS10.

Repeat the last 2 rows 6 times more, (14 rows in all). Now work across all stitches in st st for another 10 rows beginning with a knit row and ending with a purl row

Motif

Motif is worked from chart, using intarsia method, over 27 sts reading rows from right to left.

Row 1: K20, (p1, k1) 13 times, p1, k20.

Continue working from chart until row 32 is complete.

Continue in St st and vanilla until work measures 8 in (20 cm) or required length.

Shape Sleeves

Bind off 2 sts at the beginning of the next 2 rows.

Next row: K2, k2tog, knit to last 4 sts, sl 1, k1, psso, k2.

Next row. Purl.

Continue as for last 2 rows until you have 33 sts on the needle, end with RS facing for next row.

Shape Neck

K2, k2tog, k6. Turn and work on this side first.

0 = purl, / = knit, X = contrast yarn
Knit from right to left

Next row: P2tog, purl to end.
Next row: K2, k2tog, k2, k2tog.
Next row: P2tog, purl to end.
Next row: K2, k3tog.
Next row: P2tog, p1.
Next row: K2tog, fasten off.

With RS facing, slip center 13 sts onto a stitch holder for front neck. Rejoin yarn to neck edge of remaining sts, knit to last 4 sts, sl 1, k1, psso, k2. Complete to match first side, reversing all shapings.

BACK
Using US 5 (UK 9 / 3.75 mm) and vanilla, cast on 67 sts.
Work 10 rows in SS.
Change to US 6 (UK 8 / 4 mm).

Row 1: (RS) SS10, knit to last 10 sts, SS10.
Row 2: SS10, purl to last 10 sts, SS 10.
Repeat the last 2 rows 6 times more (14 rows in all).
Now work across all stitches in St st until back length matches front up to beginning of raglan shaping, ending with a purl row.

Shape Sleeves
Bind off 2 sts at the beginning of the next 2 rows.
Next row: K2, k2tog, knit to last 4 sts, sl 1, k1, psso, k2.
Next row: Purl.
Continue decreasing as set until you have 47 sts on needle, ending with a purl row.

Divide for Back Opening
Next row: (RS) k2, k2tog, k18. Turn and work on this side first.
Next row: Purl.
Continue to dec as before until you have 11 sts, ending with a purl row. Bind off.
With RS facing rejoin yarn to remaining stitches, bind off next 3 sts, knit to last 4 sts, sl 1, k1, psso, k2.
Complete to match first side, reversing all shapings.

LEFT SLEEVE
Using US 3 (UK 10 / 3.25 mm) and vanilla, cast on 37 sts.
Work in SS for 10 rows.

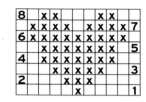

X = contrast yarn

Change to US 6 (UK 8 / 4 mm).

Row 11: K2, inc 1, knit to last 3 sts, inc 1, k2.
Continue in St st and increase as row 11 on every 4th row following until you have 47 sts on the needles. End with a purl row. Place heart. Continue to inc on every 4th row as before, taking the yarn across the back of the fabric for this motif.

Row 1: K23 vanilla, k1 rosy, k23 vanilla.

Complete heart and then continue in vanilla only, increasing until there are 59 sts on the needle. Continue in St st until work measures 8 in (20 cm) or desired length, ending with a purl row.

Shape Sleeves

Bind off 2 sts at the beginning of the next 2 rows.

Next row: K2, k2tog, knit to last 4 sts, sl 1, k1, psso, k2.

Next row: Purl

Repeat as for last 2 rows until 19 sts remain.

Purl 1 row. (RS facing for next row).

Next row: Dec 1 st at each end of next row, then bind off 4 sts at beginning of following row.

Next row: Dec 1 st at beginning of next row.

Next row: Bind off 6 sts at beginning of next row.

Bind off remaining 6 sts.

RIGHT SLEEVE

Using vanilla and US 3 (UK 10/ 3.25 mm) needles cast on 37 sts.

Work in SS for 10 rows.

Change to US 6 (UK 8 / 4 mm).

Row 11: K2, inc 1, knit to last 3 sts, inc 1, k2.
Continue in St st and increase as for row 1 on every 4th row following until there are 59 sts.

Continue in St st until work measures 8 in (20 cm) or desired length, ending on a purl row.

Shape Raglans

Bind off 2 sts at the beginning of the next 2 rows.

Next row: K2, k2tog, knit to last 4 sts, sl 1, k1, psso, k2.

Next row: Purl

Continue to decrease as on last 2 rows until 19 sts remain.

Purl 1 row.

Next row: Bind off 5 sts at beg and dec 1 st at end of next row.

Work 1 row.

Next row: Bind off 6 sts at beg and dec 1 st at end of next row.

Work 1 row. Bind off remaining 6 sts.

Finishing

Sew in all yarn ends. Press each item. Join the raglan seams with a flat seam.

BUTTON BORDER

With RS facing, using US 3 (UK 10/ 3.25 mm) needles and vanilla, starting at neck edge, pick up and k19 sts along the back opening. Work 5 rows SS. Bind off.

BUTTONHOLE BORDER

With RS facing, using US 3 (UK 10/ 3.25 mm) and vanilla, pick up and knit 19 sts, beg at base of opening. Work 1 row in SS.

Next row: Work 5 sts. [Work next 2 sts tog, yo, k5] repeat once.

Work 3 more rows SS, bind off.

NECK BORDER

With RS facing, US 3 (UK 10 / 3.25 mm) and vanilla, beg at bind-off edge of bands and pick up and knit 12 sts from left back, 16 sts from sleeve, 23 sts from front (including sts on holder for neck front), 16 sts from second sleeve, and 12 sts from right back (79 sts).

Work 1 row SS.

Next row: Work 1 st, work 2tog, yo, work in pattern to end.

Now work another 3 rows in SS. Bind off. Join side and sleeve seams neatly. Place buttonhole band over button band and sew neatly in place to bind off sts at base of opening. Sew on buttons.

Mock Cable Scarf

A simple but attractive mock cable stitch pattern adds interest to a warm, snuggly scarf. Add a fringed tassel to each end to complete the look.
This scarf is made in a soft pure wool, tweed-effect yarn in aran weight. But you could substitute any similar weight yarn, if desired.

✳✳ Intermediate

MEASUREMENTS
6 x 36 in (15 x 92 cm)

MATERIALS
◆ 3 x 50g balls Rowan Felted Tweed Aran / Worsted, 50% merino wool / 25% alpaca / 25% viscose (50g; 95 yd / 87m) Glade, shade 733
◆ Knitting needles size US 8 (UK 6 / 5 mm)
◆ Cable needle and wool needle
Gauge is not important on this piece

SPECIAL ABBREVIATION
CR3 = Slip next st onto cable needle and leave at front of work, knit next 2 sts, then knit st on cable needle.

Using US 8 (UK 6 / 5 mm) cast on 32 sts.
Row 1: (RS) P2 *k3, p2*, rep to end.
Row 2: K2, *p1, k1, p1, k2* rep from * to * to end.
Rows 3–8: Rep last 2 rows 3 more times.
Row 9: P2, *CR3, p2* rep from * to * to end.
Row 10: *As row 2.**
Repeat from ** to ** until piece measures 36 in (92 cm) ending on a WS row.
Bind off in pattern.

Finishing
Sew in yarn ends. Thread a needle with matching yarn, gather up each short end of the scarf.
Make and sew a tassel to each end.

To Make Tassels

Wind a long length of yarn around a 6 in (15 cm) wide piece of stiff card. Remove carefully from the card and tie the threads tightly together in one place. Cut the yarn opposite the tie. Fold yarn bundle in half and tie another piece of yarn tightly around the bundle a little way down from the original tie to form the tassel head. Sew a tassel to each gathered end of the scarf. Trim to tidy.

Unisex Cardigan

An easy four-row yoke pattern makes this otherwise plain cardigan a little bit different. Stockinette stitch is used for the sleeves and the main body pieces and a neat ridged twist pattern accentuates the back and front yokes. I used a neutral shade to suit a boy or girl - just change the side the buttons appear on.

✱✱ Intermediate

MEASUREMENTS

22–24 in (56–61 cm) chest; length from back neck approximately 12½ in (32 cm); sleeve seam approximately 8 in (20 cm); side seam 7 in (18 cm)

MATERIALS

- Sirdar Sublime Cashmerino, 75% extra fine merino / 20% silk / 5% cashmere
- 5 x 50 g ball Pebble, shade 006
- Knitting needles size US 5 (UK 9 / 3.75 mm) and US 6 (UK 8 / 4 mm)
- 6 matching buttons

GAUGE

22 sts x 28 rows st st = 4 in (10 cm) square when knitted using US 6 (UK 8 / 4 mm) knitting needles

SPECIAL ABBREVIATIONS

Tw2f = Knit into front of second st on needle, do not slip st off needle, knit the first st in the usual way and slip both sts off needles together.

Tw2b = Knit into back of second st on needle, do not slip st off needle, knit the first st in the usual way and slip both sts off needles together.

BACK

Using US 5 (UK 9 / 3.75 mm) and yarn, cast on 68 sts.

Work in k1, p1 rib for 8 rows.

Change to US 6 (UK 8 / 4 mm) and work in St st for 44 rows. (Adjust length here if desired.)

Shape Armholes

Bind off 6 sts at beg of next 2 rows (56 sts).

Work in pattern for yoke.

Row 1: P3, tw2f, *p4, tw2f* rep from * to * to last 3 sts, p3.

Row 2: K3, *p2, k4* to last 3 sts, p3.

Row 3: P3, tw2b, *p4, tw2b* rep from * to * to last 3 sts, p3.

Row 4: As row 2.

These 4 rows form pattern Work 36 more rows in pattern.

Shape Shoulders

Keeping pattern correct, bind off 8 sts at beg of next 4 rows.

Bind off.

LEFT FRONT

Using US 5 (UK 9 / 3.75 mm), cast on 32 sts.

Work in k1, p1 rib for 8 rows.

Change to US 6 (UK 8 / 4 mm) and work in St st for 44 rows. (Adjust length here if desired.)

Shape Armhole

(RS) Bind off 6 sts, knit to end (26 sts).

Next row: Purl.

Work in Pattern for Yoke:

Row 1: P3, tw2f, *p4, tw2f* rep from * to * to last 3 sts, p3.

Row 2: K3, *p2, k4* rep from * to * to last 5 sts, p2, k3.

Row 3: P3, tw2b, *p4, tw2b* rep from * to * to last 3 sts, p3.

Row 4: As row 2.

Work another 21 rows.

Shape Neck

Keeping pattern correct, bind off 4 sts at beg of next row.

Dec 1 st at neck edge on next 3 rows, then on following 3 alt rows.

Work 5 rows.

Shape Shoulder

Bind off 8 sts at beg of next row.

Work 1 row. Bind off remaining 8 sts.

RIGHT FRONT

Using US 5 (UK 9 / 3.75 mm), cast on
32 sts.

Work in k1, p1 rib for 8 rows.

Change to US 6 (UK 8 / 4 mm) and work
in St st for 45 rows. (Adjust length here
if desired.)

Shape Armhole

(WS) Bind off 6 sts, purl to end
(26 sts).

Work in Pattern for Yoke:

Row 1: P3, tw2f, *p4, tw2f* rep from * to *
to last 3 sts, p3.

Row 2: K3, *p2, k4* rep from * to * to last
5 sts, p2, k3.

Row 3: P3, tw2b, *p4, tw2b* rep from
* to * to last 3 sts, p3.

Row 4: As row 2

Work another 22 rows.

Shape Neck

Keeping pattern correct, bind off 4 sts at
beg of next row.

Dec 1 st at neck edge on next 3 rows, then
on following 3 alt rows.

Work 5 rows.

Shape Shoulder

Bind off 8 sts at beg of next row.

Work 1 row. Bind off remaining
8 sts.

SLEEVES

Using US 5 (UK 9 / 3.75 mm), cast on
36 sts.

Work 10 rows k1, p1 rib.

Change to US 6 (UK 8 / 4 mm) and work
4 rows St st.

Inc 1 st at each end of next and then
every following 4th row until there are
58 sts.

Work 5 rows St st. Bind off loosely.

Make 2.

NECK BAND

Join shoulder seams neatly, matching
patterns.

With RS facing and using US 5 (UK 9 /
3.75 mm), begin at left front neck edge and
pick up 20 sts along left neck side, 24 sts
across back neck and 20 sts down right
front (64 sts).

Work 6 rows in k1, p1 rib. Bind off neatly in rib.

BUTTONHOLE BAND

With RS facing and using US 5 (UK 9 / 3.75 mm), beg at base of right front for girls or left front for boys, pick up and knit 83 sts evenly all along the front edge. Work in k1, p1 rib for 3 rows.

Buttonhole row: Rib 4, *yo, work 2tog, rib 13*, rep from * to * 4 more times, yo, work 2tog, rib 2.

Work 3 more rows in rib.

Bind off firmly in rib.

BUTTON BAND

With RS facing and using US 5 (UK 9 / 3.75 mm), beg at top of neck band on left front for girls or left front for boys, pick up and knit 83 sts evenly all along the front edge. Work in k1, p1 rib for 7 rows, bind off in rib.

Finishing

Work in all ends neatly. Fold sleeves in half lengthways, mark center of sleeve top and match to center of shoulders, pin and sew sleeves in place.

Sew on buttons to correspond with buttonholes.

Striped Beach Sweater

Using cotton yarn and nautical colors make this oversized sweater for your toddler to wear on the beach as a cover up. Or team it with jeans for a cute summer look. A pocket embellished with an anchor motif completes the look.

✳✳ Intermediate

MEASUREMENTS
To fit chest 22–24 in (56–61 cm);
sleeve seam 8½ in (22 cm);.
length from back neck 14 in (36 cm)
Note Sleeve and side seams are adjustable

MATERIALS
- Rowan Pima cotton DK, 100% pima cotton
  (50g; 142 yd /130 m)
- 5 x 50 g balls Skipper, shade 062
- 3 x 50 g balls Pampas, shade 050
- 2 small buttons to match skipper yarn.
- Knitting needles size US 5 and 6
  (UK 8 and 9 / 3.75 and 4 mm)
- 2 x stitch holders

GAUGE
22 sts x 30 rows St st= 4 in (10 cm) square
using US 6 (UK 8 / 4 mm) knitting needles

BACK

Using US 5 (UK 9 / 3.75 mm) and
pampas, cast on 70 sts.
Work 8 rows in garter stitch.
Change to US 6 (UK 8 / 4 mm) and work
in St st stripes of 6 rows skipper and
2 rows pampas until work measures 14 in
(35 cm), ending on a purl row.

Shape Shoulders

Bind off 11 sts at beg of next 2 rows and 10
sts at beg of following 2 rows.
Leave rem 28 sts on a stitch holder.

FRONT

Work as for back until piece measures
12 in (30 cm).
Keeping continuity of the striped
sequence

Shape Neck:

Next row: K28, turn and work on these sts
only, dec 1 st at neck edge on next
7 rows (21 sts).
Continue straight until front matches
back to shoulder ending at side edge.
Bind off 11 sts at beg of next row.
Work 1 row and bind off.

With RS facing, slip center 14 sts onto
stitch holder. Rejoin yarn and knit to end.
Complete to match first side.

SLEEVES

Using US 5 (UK 9 / 3.75 mm) and
pampas, cast on 42 sts.
Work in garter stitch for 6 rows.
Change to US 6 (UK 8 / 4 mm) and St st
and work in stripes as for back and front,
but inc 1 st at each end of 5th and every
following 6th row until 60 sts.
Continue straight until sleeve measures
8¾ in (22 cm). Bind off loosely.
Make 2.

NECKBAND

Join right shoulder seam.
Using US 5 (UK 9 / 3.75 mm) and
pampas, pick up and knit 15 st down left
front neck, knit across center front sts
from stitch holder, then 15 sts up right
side of neck, finally work across back
neck sts from stitch holder (72 sts).

Work 8 rows in garter stitch, bind off firmly.

Join left shoulder seam for 2 in (5 cm).

BUTTONHOLE BAND

Using US 5 (UK 9 / 3.75 mm) and pampas and with RS of front facing, starting at shoulder edge, pick up and knit 13 sts along the rest of the shoulder seam.

Next row: Knit.

Next row: K3, yo twice, k2tog, k3, yo twice, k2tog, k3.

Next row: Knit, knitting into yo of previous row.

Next row: Knit. Bind off.

BUTTON BAND

Work as buttonhole band, omitting the yo twice on buttonholes row and starting at the neck edge of the back.

POCKET

Using US 6 (UK 8 / 4 mm) and pampas, cast on 24 sts.

Knit 6 rows in garter stitch.

Next row: Knit.

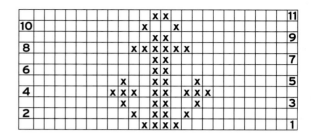

Next row: K2, p20, k2.

Repeat last 2 rows twice more.

Using stranding technique begin anchor motif from chart using a small ball of skipper and at the same time working 2 edge sts as before in garter stitch.

Row 1: K10 pampas, k4 skipper, k10 pampas.
Continue from chart until all 11 rows are
complete. Break yarn.
Next row: K2, p20, k2.
Work another 4 rows in St st with garter
stitch edging.
Work 6 rows garter stitch.
Bind off firmly.

Finishing

Sew in any loose ends. Fold sleeves in half
lengthways and mark the center top of
the sleeve. Match the marked point to the
center of the shoulder seam. Pin and sew
in place. Join side and underarm seams on
each side.
Sew buttons on to correspond with
buttonholes.
Pin and sew the pocket in place on one side
of the sweater front.

Moccasin Slipper Socks

Just two balls of this soft chunky yarn is all it takes to make these cozy slipper socks. They are sure to keep tiny toes toasty warm and snug. The two-row pattern is not too difficult to follow and gives a chunky appearance to the finished fabric. A separate sole is knitted and sewn on to provide added depth to the underside of the slipper.

✳✳ Intermediate

To fit 3–5 years

MEASUREMENTS

Length of sole 5 in (13 cm); height from sole to top 6 in (15 cm)

MATERIALS

◆ Wendy Norse Chunky Yarn / Bulky 50% wool / 50% acrylic (50g; 87 yd / 80 m)
◆ 1 x 50 g ball Drift, shade 2700
◆ 1 x 50 g ball in Aurora, shade 2706
◆ Knitting needles size US 8 (UK 6 / 5 mm)

GAUGE

16 sts x 24 rows st st = 4 in (10 cm) square when knitted using US 8 (UK 5 / 5 mm) knitting needles

Note For safety reasons these slippers are for indoor use on carpets only. If you wish you could purchase some Jiffy Grip fabric and sew it to the sole of the slipper to make the moccasin suitable for use on uncarpeted floors. Jiffy Grip fabric is available via the internet.

Tip The yarn is very soft and splits easily. When sewing up use short lengths of yarn and don't pull too tightly.

SPECIAL ABBREVIATIONS

KB1 = K1 below; knit into the next stitch on the row below the stitch on the needle.

Using US 8 (UK 6 / 5 mm) and drift, cast on 29 sts.
Work 5 rows garter stitch
Row 6: Knit using drift.
Row 7: *K1, kB1* repeat from * to * to end of row.
Row 8: Knit using aurora.
Row 9: K2, *kB1, k1* rep from * to * to last.
Rows 6–9 form the pattern and are repeated. Continue in pattern, alternating color every 2 rows for another 26 rows.

Divide for Foot

Keeping continuity of the pattern:
Next row: Pattern 19, turn.
Next row: Pattern 9, turn.
Continue in pattern on these center 9 sts for another 16 rows.
Break yarn.
Rejoin yarn to sts on right-hand needle.
Pick up and k8 sts up right side of foot, pattern across sts of toe, pick up and k8 sts down left side of foot, then work across remaining 10 sts on left-hand needle (45 sts).
Next row: Knit.
Work 10 rows in garter stitch using drift.

Decrease for Foot

Next row: K1, k2tog, k14, k2tog, k7, k2tog, k14, k2tog, k1 (41 sts).
Next row: Knit.
Next row: K1, k2tog, k12, k2tog, k7, k2tog, k12, k2tog, k1 (37 sts).
Next row: Knit.
Next row: K1, k2tog, k10, k2tog, k7, k2tog, k10, k2tog, k1 (33 sts).
Next row: Knit.
Next row: K1, k2tog, k8, k2tog, k7, k2tog, k8, k2tog, k1 (29 sts).
Bind off.

SOLE

Work in garter stitch. Make 2.
Using aurora and size US 8 (UK 6/ 5 mm) cast on 6 sts.
Knit 1 row.
Inc 1 st at each end of next and foll alt rows until you have 12 sts.

Work 8 rows.
Dec 1 stitch at each end of next row.
Work 6 rows.
Inc 1 stitch at each end of next row.
Work 12 rows.
Dec 1 stitch at each end of next and foll
alt rows until 6 sts remain. Bind off. (This
is the toe end.)

Finishing

Sew in ends. Join leg and foot seam.
Pin sole in place, matching toe to toe of
slipper and making sure that the rows on
each side of the foot are even. Sew neatly
in place all around.
Take lengths of both yarn colors and wind
them into a tassel. Wind yarn around the
top firmly and secure with a few stitches.
Make another tassel to match. Sew to the
sides of the slippers.

Scandinavian Sweater and Hat

This beautiful set is not for the faint-hearted! The patterning, although not complicated, requires plenty of concentration when following charts and shaping neck and sleeves. I have stranded the yarn not in use across the back of the work but unless you are experienced at doing this then weaving the yarn in on every third or fourth stitch might prove easier.

✳✳ Intermediate

SWEATER MEASUREMENTS
Chest 22-24 / 24-26 in (56-61 / 61-66 cm); length from back neck (adjustable) 13 / 16 in (34 / 40 cm)
sleeve: (adjustable) 11 / 13 in (29 / 34 cm)

SWEATER MATERIALS
• Rico Essentials Merino DK, 100% merino extrafine superwash (50g; 131 yd / 120 m)
• 7 x 50 g balls in jeans (blue), shade 27 (A)
• 2 x 50 g balls in ecru, shade 60 (B)
• Knitting needles, size US 5 and 7 (UK 7 and 9 / 3.75 and 4.5 mm)
• Stitch holder

HAT MEASUREMENTS
Circumference 16–18 in (41–46 cm) when slightly stretched

GAUGE
22 sts and 28 rows st st = 4 in (10 cm) square using US 7 (UK 7 / 4.5 mm) knitting needles

Note Work the back and sleeves first to familiarize yourself with the snowflake pattern, you will then find it easier to place and work the reindeer chart AT THE SAME TIME, when working the front of the sweater.

BACK SWEATER

With US 5 (UK 9 / 3.75 mm) using ecru, cast on 80 (86) sts.

Work 2 rows in k2, p2 rib.

Change to blue and continue in k2, p2 rib for another 14 (16) rows (dec 1 st in the center of the last row) 79 (85) sts.

Change to US 7 (UK 7 / 4.5 mm) knitting and St st. Work pattern from chart below

left and then begin working from chart below right, reading rows from right to left for knit and left to right for purl. Continue until work measures 13 / 15¾ in (34 / 40 cm).

Shape Shoulders

Bind off 3 sts at beg of next 4 rows. Then 8 (9) sts at beg of following 4 rows. Leave remaining sts on stitch holder.

FRONT SWEATER

Work as for back until piece is 32 (36) rows less than back to shoulder shaping, ending on a WS row.

Place reindeer chart. Join in separate balls of contrast as needed and read rows from right to left.

Row 1: (Knit.) Pattern 19 (23), work first row of chart, pattern 19 (23).

Continue until 18 rows of chart are complete and AT THE SAME TIME keeping continuity of the snowflake patterning on the 19 (23) sts at each side.

Work another 4 (6) rows pattern.

Neck Shaping

Pattern 26 (29), turn and continue on

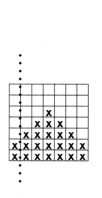

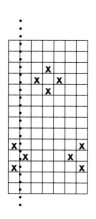

these sts only.

Dec 1 st at neck edge on next and every following alt row until 22 (24) sts remain.

Work another 4 rows.

Shape Shoulders

Bind off 3 sts at beg of next and following alt row. Bind off 8 (9) sts at beg of following 2 alt rows. Slip center 27 (27) sts onto a stitch holder.

Work other side of neck to match, reversing shaping rows.

SLEEVES

Using US 5 (UK 9 / 3.75 mm) and ecru, cast on 44 (50) sts

Work 2 rows k2, p2 rib.

Change to blue and work another 14 (16) rows in k2, p2 rib. Dec 1 st in center of last row.

Change to US 7 (UK 7 / 4.5 mm) and working in St st, begin working from border pattern chart (opposite page, left) and then snowflake chart (opposite page, right) as before, taking care to work increased sts into pattern.

Inc 1 st at each end of the next and following 4th (5th) rows until there are

61 (67) sts on needle.

Continue straight in pattern until work measures 11 (13) in / 29 (34) cm ending on a purl row. Bind off.

NECKBAND

Join right shoulder seam. Using US 5 mm (UK 9 / 3.75) and main color, pick up and knit 13 (17) sts down side of neck, 27 sts from front neck, 13 (17) sts from other side of neck and 27 (29) sts from back neck.

Work 9 rows k2, p2 rib.

Join in contrast color and work 4 rows k2, p2 rib.

Rejoin main color and work another 8 rows k2, p2 rib. Bind off loosely.

Finishing

Work in all ends neatly. Lightly press all pieces using a warm iron and a damp cloth. Join left shoulder seam. Fold neckband in half to wrong side, catch down making sure you maintain the elasticity of the ribbing.

Fold sleeve in half lengthways, mark the center of the top sleeve and match it to shoulder seam. Pin and sew in place neatly with back stitch. Repeat for other sleeve. Sew side and sleeve seams, matching patterning.

HAT

Using US 5 (UK 9 / 3.75 mm) and contrast color, cast on 110 sts.

Work 2 rows, k2, p2 rib. Change to main color and work in k2, p2 rib for another 3 in (8 cm). Dec 1 st on last row (109 sts). Change to US 7 (UK 7 / 4.5 mm) and contrast color, work 2 rows St st.

Edge Pattern

Row 1: *K1A, k5B*, repeat to last st, k1A.

Row 2: *P2A, *p3B, p3A* repeat to last 2 sts, p2A.

Row 3: K3A, *k1B, k5A* repeat to last 4 sts, k1B, k3A.

Work 3 rows st st in main color.

Work from chart B. Continue in snowflake pattern until work measures 4–4½ in (10–12) cm) from start of St st ending on a purl row. Continue in main color only.

Crown Shaping

Row 1: K1, (k2tog, k4) to end.

Row 2: Purl.

Row 3: K1. (k2tog, k3) to end.

Row 4: Purl.

Row 5: K1, (k2tog, k2) to end.

Row 6: Purl.

Row 7: K2, (k2tog, k1) to end.

Row 8: Purl.

Row 9: K1, (k2tog) to end.

Row 10: Purl.

Repeat rows 9 and 10 once.

Break off yarn and run through remaining stitches on needle, draw up tight and fasten off.

Finishing

Sew side seam matching pattern as you do. Reverse seam on turn back. Make a large pompom using both colors. Sew securely to center of crown.

Finnley the Fish

Who can resist this cute and fabulous toy fish? With his bright colors
and multi-textures he will make any young child happy. Made using pure wool
and simple knitting stitches he can be knitted in just a couple of evenings.
Use any DK yarns from your stash. Sew him up very firmly,
especially when attaching the eyes and fins.

❋❋ **Intermediate**

MEASUREMENTS

13 in (32 cm) from tip of nose to tail.

MATERIALS

- Patons Fairytale Color 4 me DK, 100% wool
  (50g; 98 yd / 90 m) in the following colors:
- 1 x 50 g Lilac blue, shade 4965
- 1 x 50 g Yellow, shade 4960
- 1 x 50 g Random stripe, shade 4970
- 1 x 50 g Orange, shade 4951
- 1 x 50 g Lime green, shade 4952
- 1 x 50 g Pink, shade 4953
- Oddments of White, shade 4973 and Black
  shade 4969, for eyes

- Knitting needles size US 6 (UK 8 / 4 mm)
- Crochet hook size US G/8 (UK 8 / 4 mm)
- Fiberfil toy stuffing
- 2 x small circles of black and 2 small circles
  of white felt

SPECIAL ABBREVIATION

MB = Make Bobble. K4 times into next st,
knitting alternately into the back and the front
of the stitch, turn, knit 4, turn, p4, slip second,
third, fourth stitch over first stitch.

Skpo = Slip 1, knit 1, pass slipped stitch over

BODY

Begin at the nose.

Using US 6 (UK 8 / 4 mm) and yellow, cast on 4 sts.

Row 1: Knit.

Row 2: Purl.

Row 3: Inc in each stitch, knit to end (8 sts).

Row 4: Purl.

Row 5: Knit.

Row 6: Purl.

Row 7: Inc in each stitch, knit to end (16 sts).

Work 7 rows St st.

Row 15: *K1, inc in next st* to end (24 sts).

Work 7 rows St st.

Row 23: *K2, inc in next st* to end (32 sts).

Work 7 rows St st.

Change to green.

Row 31: *K2, inc in next st* to last 2 sts, k2 (42 sts).

Row 32: Knit.

Work 5 rows St st.

Row 38: Knit.

Change to lilac blue (B) but work bobbles in contrast color, joining in new ones as needed. Strand the contrast yarn across the back of the work on the bobble rows. Work contrast bobbles in orange, pink and yellow.

Beginning with a knit row, work 4 rows st st.

Row 43: Join in contrast and k6B, MB, *k5B, MB * to last 5 sts, k5B.

Beg with a purl row work 7 rows St st.

Row 51: Join in contrast and k3B, MB, *k5B, MB* to last 2 sts, k2B.

Beg with a purl row work 7 rows St st.

Row 59: Join in contrast and k6B, MB, *k5B, MB* to last 5 sts, k5B.

Continue in lilac blue yarn only.

Row 60: Purl.

Row 61: Knit.

Row 62: Purl.

Row 63: K2, *skpo, k2* to end (32 sts).

Beg with a purl row, work 3 rows St st.

Change to orange.

Knit 2 rows.

Work 2 rows in St st.

Row 71: *K2 skpo* to end (24 sts).

Beg with a purl row, work 2 rows St st.

Row 74: Knit.

Work 2 rows St st.

Row 77: *K2 skpo* to end (18 sts).

Beg with a purl row, work 2 rows St st.

Row 80: Knit.

Work 2 rows St st.

Row 83: * K1, skpo* to end (12 sts).

Beg with a purl row, work 3 rows St st.

Bind off.

Make 2.

TAIL

Work in garter stitch.

Using US 6 (UK 8 / 4 mm) and random stripe yarn, cast on 12 sts.

Knit 2 rows.

Inc 1 st at each end of next and every following 3rd row until there are 26 sts.

Knit 4 rows.

Dec 1 st at each end of next and every following 3rd row until 12 sts remain.

Knit 2 rows. Bind off.

Fold tail in half, sew the sides together leaving the base open. Lightly stuff, then stich the opening closed. Stitch a line of yarn through the center of the tail from top to base, draw this up to give the indentation.

BACK FIN

Work in garter stitch.

Using US 6 (UK 8 / 4 mm) and random stripe yarn, cast on 26 sts.

Knit 2 rows.

Row 3: Inc in first st, knit to last 2 sts, k2tog.

Row 4: Knit.

Repeat the last 2 rows 9 times more.

Knit 4 rows straight.

Next row: K2tog, knit to last st, increase in this st.

Next row: Knit

Repeat last 2 rows 9 times more,
Knit 2 rows. Bind off.
Fold fin in half, sew short side seams together. Lightly stuff and then sew seam at base. Take matching yarn and sew some lines along the length of the fin to give detail.

SIDE FINS
Work in garter stitch
Using US 6 (UK 8 / 4 mm) and random stripe yarn, cast on 6 sts.
Knit 2 rows.
Row 3: Inc in first and last st.
Row 4: Knit.
Repeat last 2 rows until there are 12 sts.
Work 10 rows straight.
Next row: Dec 1 st at each end of next and following alt rows until 6 sts remain.
Bind off.
Make 2.

LIPS
Work in St st.
Using US 6 (UK 8 / 4 mm) and pink yarn, cast on 9 sts.

Work 2 rows in St st.
Inc 1 st at each end of next and every following alt row until there are 19 sts.
Work 3 rows in St st.
Dec 1 st at each end of next and following alt rows until 9 sts remain.
Work 2 rows St st. Bind off.
Fold the piece in half lengthways with the RS together. Sew along the center line to form the lip crease. Fold each side back on itself to meet at the center stitched line. Sew the lips in place but add a little stuffing to pad them out.

EYES
Note Cut 2 circles of felt for each eye or crochet them as follows:

Inner Eye
(Make 2) Using a size US G/8 (UK 8 / 4 mm) crochet hook and black yarn make 3 ch, work 6 sc into second ch from hook. Join with a slip stitch.
Next row: Work 2 sc into each sc all around.**
Fasten off.

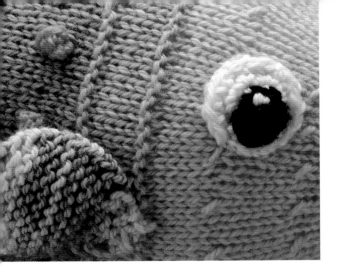

Outer Eye

(Make 2) Work as inner eye to ** but use white instead of black.

Next row: Work 1 sc into each sc all around. Fasten off.

Place inner eye onto outer eye and stitch together.

Finishing

Sew in all yarn ends. With right sides together, sew main body pieces together, matching stripes. Leave an opening at the mouth and tail to turn and stuff the fish. Turn right side out, stuff quite firmly giving the body a rounded shape. When you are happy with the result, sew up the two openings.

Sew the eyes in place on each side of the face.

With black yarn embroider an eyebrow above each eye, if you like.

Pin the side fins to each side of the fish ensuring that they are level. Sew the tops of the fins in place, making a small pleat in the fin to add fullness.

Sew the back fin firmly on the center back of the fish, catching it down on each side.

Sew the tail onto the body.

Pin the lips in place, curving them slightly to fit to the contours of the body.

When you are happy with the position, stitch in place.

Lace and Cable Hat and Mittens

Marbled yarn, a sweet lace and cable stitch are combined to make this chunky warm hat for little girls. A fluffy pompom adds a finishing touch. Team with mittens to make a super cute set for winter outings.

✳✳ Intermediate (hat) * Beginner (mittens)

MEASUREMENTS
To fit 3 (5) years (hat). The pattern is quite stretchy.
Mittens fit size 3–5 years

MATERIALS
◆ James Brett Baby Marble yarn DK, 100% acrylic (100g; 293 yd / 268 m)
◆ 1 x 100 g ball in shade BM11
◆ Knitting needles size US 8 (UK 6 / 5 mm)

GAUGE
19 sts x 24 rows st st = 4 in (10 cm) square

SPECIAL ABBREVIATIONS
C6B = Cable 6 sts to the back: Slip first 3 sts onto a cable needle, leave at back of work, knit next 3 sts, then knit the 3 sts from the cable needle.
M1 = Make 1 stitch by picking up the strand that lies between the stitch you are working and the next stitch on the needle, and knitting into the back of it.
Skpo = Slip 1, knit 1, pass slipped stitch over.
Tip There is sufficient yarn to make the girls' hat and mittens, or two pairs of mittens.

Using US 8 (UK 6 / 5 mm) and yarn, cast on 94 sts.

Work in k2, p2 rib for 16 rows, dec 1 st on last row (93 sts).

Begin Pattern

Next row: (RS) *P3, k2tog, yo, k2, yo, skpo* rep from * to * to last 3 sts, p3.

Next row: *K3, p6*, rep from * to * last 3 sts, k3.

Repeat the last 2 rows three more times.

Next row: *P3, C6B* rep from * to * to last 6 sts, p3.

Next row: *K3, p6*, rep from * to * to last 3 sts, k3.

The last 10 rows form the pattern. Repeat them twice more, ending on a WS row.

Decrease for Crown

Row 1: *P1, p2tog, k6*, to last 3 sts, p2tog, p1.

Row 2 and all following even rows: Knit all knit sts and purl all purl sts.

Row 3: P2, *k2, k2tog, k2, p2tog * rep to last 2 sts, p2.

Row 5: P2, *K2tog, k1, k2tog, p1*, rep to last 2 sts, p2.

Row 7: P2, *sl 1, k2tog, psso, p1* to last 4 sts, sl 1, k2tog, psso, p2.

Row 9: P1, *k2tog*, rep across row, to last 2 sts, p2tog.

Break yarn and run through stitches on needle, gather up and secure. Sew side seam neatly.

Make a large pompom and sew to the top of the hat securely.

RIGHT MITTEN

Using US 8 (UK 6 / 5 mm), cast on 30 sts.

Work in k2, p2 rib for 18 rows.

Work 2 rows st st **

Shape Thumb

Next row: K16, m1, k1, m1, k13.

Next and following alt rows: Purl.

Next row: K16, m1, k3, m1, k13.

Next row: K16, m1, k5, m1, k13

Next row: K16, m1, k7,m1, k13.

Next row: Purl (38 sts).

Work Thumb

Next row: K25, turn, cast on 1 st.

Next row: P10, turn, cast on 1 st.

***Work 6 rows in St st on these 11sts.

Next row: K2tog across row to last st, k1.

Break yarn and thread through sts, draw

up and fasten off. Sew the thumb seam. With RS facing, rejoin yarn. Pick up and knit 2 sts from the base of the thumb, knit to end of row (31 sts).

Next row: Purl.

Work 10 rows St st ending in purl.

Shape Top

Row 1: K1, k2tog, k10, k2tog, k1, k2tog, k10, k2tog, k1 (27 sts).

Row 2: Purl.

Row 3: K1, k2tog, k8, k2tog, k1, k2tog, k8, k2tog, k1 (23 sts).

Row 4: Purl.

Row 5: K1, k2tog, k6, k2tog, k1, k2tog, k6, k2tog, k1 (19 sts).

Row 6: Purl.

Row 7: K1, k2tog, k4, k2tog, k1, k2tog, k4, k2tog, k1 (15 sts).

Row 8: Purl. Bind off.

LEFT MITTEN

Work as for Right Mitten to **

Shape Thumb

Row 1: K13, m1, k1, m1, k16.

Row 2 and all following even rows: Purl.

Row 3: K13, m1, k3, m1, k16.

Row 5: K13, m1, k5, m1, k16.

Row 7: K13, m1, k7, m1, k16.

Row 8: Purl.

Work Thumb

Next row: K22, turn.

Next row: P9, turn.

Complete as for Right Mitten from ***

Finishing

The purl side is the right side of the mitten. Sew side seam and top of mitten. Fold back cuffs.

Make two small pompoms and attach firmly to the side seams on both mittens, catching the cuffs in place with a few stitches as you work.

Cable Vest

Unusual stitch patterning along with a lovely soft bamboo yarn give this cute cabled vest a modern look. Make the little man in your life look dressed up for special outings when you pair the vest with a collared shirt or go for a casual look with a long sleeved T-shirt and jeans. Take care to keep the pattern lined up when shaping the armholes and neck.

✳✳✳ Experienced

MEASUREMENTS

Chest 22–24 in (56–61 cm);
length from back neck 12 in (30 cm)

MATERIALS

◆ Sirdar Snuggly Baby Bamboo DK,
80% bamboo viscose, 20% wool (50g; 105 yd
  / 95 m)
◆ 5 x 50 g balls groovy green, shade 122
◆ Knitting needles size US 5 and 6
  (UK 8 and 9 / 3.75 and 4 mm)
◆ 2 stitch holders
◆ Safety pin

GAUGE

22 sts x 28 rows st st = 4 in (10 cm) square
using US 6 (UK 8 / 4 mm) knitting needles

Tip Mark down the rows as you work them
when decreasing for the V-neck shaping, so
that you won't forget which row you are on if
you leave your work.

BACK

Using US 5 (UK 9 / 3.75 mm) and yarn, cast on 68 sts.

Work in k2, p2 rib for 12 rows. Inc 1 st in center of last row (69 sts).

Change to US 6 (UK 8 / 4 mm) and begin pattern.

Row 1: (RS) *K5, p3* rep from * to * to last 5 sts, k5.

Row 2: P5, *k3, p5* repeat from * to * to end.

Rows 3 and 4: as rows 1 and 2.

Row 5: K1, *p3, k5*, rep from * to * to last 4 sts, p3, k1.

Row 6: P1, *k3, p5* rep from * to * to last 4 sts, k3, p1.

Rows 7 and 8: As rows 5 and 6.

These 8 rows form pattern and are repeated throughout.

Continue in pattern for another 40 rows.

Keeping continuity of the pattern

Shape Armholes as follows:

Bind off 4 sts at beg of next 2 rows.***

Dec 1 st at each end of every row until 51 sts remain.

Continue straight in pattern for another 32 rows, ending on a WS row.

Shape Shoulders

Bind off 7 sts at beg of next 2 rows, and 8 sts at beg of following 2 rows. Leave remaining 21 sts on a holder.

FRONT

Work as back to *** (61 sts).

Next row: K2tog, pattern 28, turn and work on these sts for first side of neck. Leave remaining sts on a holder.

*Keeping pattern correct dec 1 st at armhole edge on next 4 rows and AT THE SAME TIME dec 1 st at neck edge on next and every following 3rd row until 15 sts remain. Work a few rows straight until front matches back to shoulder ending at armhole edge.

Shape Shoulder

Bind off 8 sts, pattern to end.

Next row: Pattern to end.

Next row: Bind off remaining 7 sts.*

Slip center st onto safety pin. Return to sts on holder and rejoin yarn.

Next row: Pattern 28, k2tog.

Work from * to * as for first side of neck.

Join right shoulder seams.

NECK BAND

Using US 5 (UK 9 / 3.75 mm), rejoin yarn
and pick up and knit 40 sts down left side
of neck, 1 st from center safety pin, 40 sts
up other side of neck, then knit sts from
back neck (102 sts).

Work in k2, p2 rib for 6 rows and AT THE
SAME TIME, keeping rib sequence correct,
dec 1 st at each side of center V st on
every row, knitting or purling the center
V stitch as you do. Bind off fairly loosely.

Armhole Edging

Join other shoulder seam and neck band.
Using US 5 (UK 9 / 3.75 mm), rejoin yarn
and with right side facing, pick up and
knit 72 sts around complete armhole (36
sts from each half.) Work 6 rows k2, p2
rib and bind off firmly. Work the other
armhole edging in the same way.

Join side seams neatly matching pattern
rows.

Braided Hairband

Make your fashion-conscious little girl a headband using a luxurious kid mohair and lambswool mix. Add a bow with a butterfly button to complete the look. You could knit this project in a weekend.

✳ **Easy**

MEASUREMENTS
To fit 2-4 years old

MATERIALS
- Rowan Kid Classic
- 1 x 50 g ball feather, shade 828
- 1 x 50 g ball tea rose, shade 854
- 1 x 50 g ball drought, shade 876
- Butterfly button
- Knitting needles size US 6 (UK 7 / 4.5 mm)

The head band is made in three strips, which are braided together.

Using feather and US 6 (UK 7 / 4.5 mm), cast on 14 sts.
Work in St st, beginning with a knit row, and continue until strip measures 21 in (53 cm). Bind off.
Make 1 strip using tea rose and 1 strip using drought.

BOW
Using tea rose and US 6 (UK 7 / 4.5 mm), cast on 8 sts.
Work in garter stitch for 8 in (20 cm). Bind off.

Finishing

Secure the ends of the strips together
with some matching yarn. Braid the strips
neatly and evenly. Secure the ends.
To join the band into a circle loosen each
end of the strips then weave them inside
each other to give the braid continuity.
Tuck in the ends and sew in place.
To make the bow, join the two short ends
of the strip together. Fold in half with the

join at the center back. With a needle
and matching yarn, thread the yarn
through the center of the bow from top to
bottom, draw up to gather the strip and
accentuate the bow. Sew firmly in place.
Sew the bow to the headband to cover
the join. Stitch the butterfly button to the
center of the bow.

Puff-sleeve Angora Cardigan

This adorable cardigan is made in sumptuous angora and lambswool and weighs very little. The colors available are just stunning so you can chose subtle shades or pick more vibrant tones. A pretty Fair Isle flower pattern decorates the lower part of the cardigan, which is worked in one piece up to the armholes.

❋❋❋ **Experienced**

MEASUREMENTS

Chest 22–24 in (56–61 cm);
length from underarm 8 in (20 cm)
sleeve seam 2 in (5 cm);
length from back neck 12 in (30 cm)

MATERIALS

- Orkney Angora 50/50 DK, 50% angora/
  50% lambswool (50g; 218 yd / 199 m)
info@orkneyangora.co.uk
- 2 x 50 g balls beige
- 1 x 50 g ball blackberry
- 1 x 50 g ball heather
- Knitting needles size US 3 and 6

(UK 10 and 8 / 3.25 and 4 mm)
- 2 stitch holders
- 5 flower buttons

GAUGE

24 sts x 26 rows st st = 4 in (10 cm) square
worked on US 6 (UK 8 / 4 mm) needles

The back and fronts are knitted in one piece to the armholes.
Using US 5 (UK 9 / 3.75 mm) and blackberry, cast on 144 sts
Work 2 rows k1, p1 rib.
Change to beige and work 8 rows k1, p1 rib.
Change to US 6 (UK 8 / 4 mm) and work 4 rows St st in beige beginning with a knit row. Joining in colors as indicated from chart, work as follows:
Next row: K3 beige, *work 6-stitch repeat from chart* between dotted lines, to last 3 sts, k3 beige.
Work next 5 rows from chart.
Work 6 rows St st in beige.
Next row: K6 beige, *work 6-stitch repeat from chart* to last 6 sts, k6 beige.
Work next 5 rows from chart.
Work 6 rows St st in beige.
Next row: K3 beige, *work 6-stitch repeat from chart* to last 3 sts, k3 beige.
Work next 5 rows from chart.
Work 6 rows St st in beige.
Next 2 rows: Using heather, work in garter st.

Next 2 rows: Using blackberry, work in garter st.
Next 2 rows: Using beige, work 2 rows St st.
Break blackberry and heather and continue in beige only.
Divide for Back and Fronts
Next row: K33, bind off 6 sts, k66, bind off 6 sts, k33.
Next row: P33, slip these sts onto a stitch holder for left front. Rejoin yarn. Purl 66 sts for back. Leave remaining 33 sts on another stitch holder for right front.

BACK
Dec 1 st at each end of the next 3 rows. Dec 1 st at each end of the next and following alt rows until there are 54 sts. Continue on these sts in St st until work measures 5 in (13 cm) ending with a purl row.
Shape Shoulders
With the RS facing, bind off 6 sts, k10 (including the st already on the needle after bind off), turn and bind off 3 sts, purl to end.

Bind off remaining sts.

LEFT FRONT

Return sts for left front to needle.
Dec 1 st at armhole edge on next 3 rows,
then on the following 3 alt rows (27 sts).
Work straight until 19 rows less than back
to shoulder shaping ending on a RS row.

Shape Neck

Bind off 6 sts at beg of next row.
Dec 1 st at neck edge on next 3 rows.
Dec 1 st on next and following 3 alt rows,
then on following 4th row at neck edge.
Work 3 rows ending on a WS row.

Shape Shoulders

Bind off 5 sts at beg of next row.
Purl I row. Bind off.

RIGHT FRONT

Return remaining stitches on holder
to needle.
Dec 1 st at armhole edge on next 3 rows,
then on the following 3 alt rows (27 sts).
Work straight until 18 rows less than back
to shoulder shaping ending on a WS row.

Shape Neck

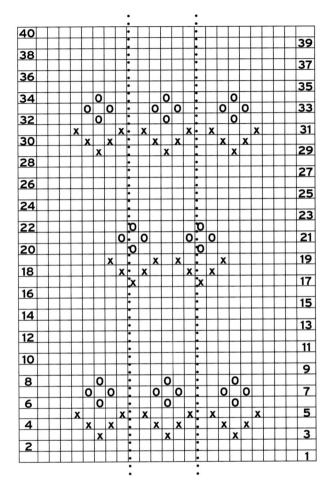

Bind off 6 sts at beg of next row.
Dec 1 st at neck edge on next 3 rows.
Dec 1 st on next and following 3 alt rows,
then on following 4th row at neck edge.

Work 3 rows ending on a RS row.

Shape Shoulders

Bind off 5 sts at beg of next row.

Purl 1 row and bind off.

SLEEVES

Using US 3 (UK 10 / 3.25 mm) and
blackberry, cast on 63 sts.

Row 1: *K1, p1* rep from * to * to last st, k1.

Row 2: *P1, k1* rep from * to * to last st, p1.

Change to beige.

Work 2 rows rib as above.

Change to US 6 (UK 8 / 4 mm)
knitting needles.

Inc row: K17, inc in each of next 28 sts, k17
(90 sts).

Work 7 rows St st.

Shape Top

Bind off 3 sts at beg of next 2 rows.

Dec 1 st at each end of next 5 rows, then
on the following 3 alt rows.

Dec 1 st at each end of every row until
42 sts remain, ending on a knit row.

Next row: P3tog across row.

Bind off firmly.

Join shoulder seams neatly.

Make 2.

NECKBAND

Using US 3 (UK 10 / 3.25 mm) and beige,
begin at the right front edge, pick up and
knit 19 sts up right front neck, 30 sts from
back neck and 19 sts down left front neck
(68 sts).

Work in k1, p1 rib for 6 rows.

Change to blackberry and work 2 rows of
k1, p1 rib. Bind off neatly in rib.

BUTTON BAND

Using US 3 (UK 10 / 3.25 mm) and
blackberry, begin at top of left front band
and pick up and knit 79 sts evenly down
entire front.
Work 1 row in k1, p1 rib.
Change to beige and work 6 rows in
k1, p1 rib.
Change to blackberry and work 1 row
k1, p1 rib. Bind off in rib.

BUTTONHOLE BAND

Using US 3 (UK 10 / 3.25 mm) and
blackberry, begin at base of right front,
pick up and knit 79 sts evenly along
entire front and neck band.
Work 1 row k1, p1 rib.
Change to beige and work 2 rows in
k1, p1 rib.
Buttonhole row: K4, bind off 2 sts, *k15
(counting the st left on needles after
binding off) bind off 2 sts*, repeat from
* to * 3 more times, k4.
Next row: Work in rib, cast on 2 sts over
each of the buttonholes made in previous
row.

Work 2 more rows k1, p1 rib in beige.
Change to blackberry and work 1 row in
rib as set.
Bind off in rib.

Finishing

Sew in any loose ends of yarns.
Join seams.
Pin sleeve in place around armhole,
easing fullness to fit evenly around the
top section. Sew in place. Repeat with the
other sleeve.
Sew buttons on to correspond with
buttonholes.

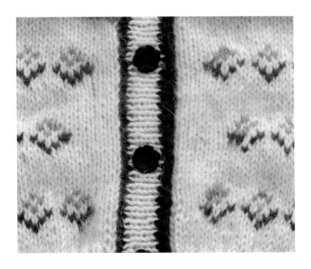

Puff-sleeve Angora Cardigan

Boys Cable Hat and Mittens

Knit this chunky cable hat for the little guy in your life. It will keep him snug and warm while he plays outside during the colder weather. The pattern stitch is quite simple to follow and by knitting into the back of the stitches it gives extra definition to the cable detail. Team the hat with matching mittens.

✳✳ Intermediate

MEASUREMENTS
To fit 3–5 years. The pattern is quite stretchy.

MATERIALS
◆ James Brett Marble yarn DK, 100% acrylic (100g; 293 yd / 268 m)
◆ 1 x 100g ball shade MT17
◆ Knitting needle size US 8 (UK 6 / 5 mm)
◆ Cable needle

GAUGE
19 sts x 24 rows st st= 4 in (10 cm) square using knitting needles

SPECIAL ABBREVIATIONS
KB1 = Knit into the back of the stitch.
C6Bk = Slip first 3 sts onto a cable needle, leave at back of work, KB1, p1, KB1 over next 3 sts, now KB1, p1, KB1 over the 3 sts from the cable needle.

Note There will be sufficient yarn to make both the boys hat and mittens, or two pairs of mittens.

Using US 8 (UK 6 / 5 mm), cast on 94 sts
Work in k2, p2 rib for 16 rows, dec 1 st on
last row (93 sts).

Next row: (RS) *KB1, p1, [KB1 (twice)], p1,
KB1* rep from * to * to last 3 sts (p3).

Next row: *K3, p1, k1, p2, k1, p1 * rep from
* to * last 3 sts, k3.

Repeat the last 2 rows three more times.

Next row: *P3, C6Bk* rep from * to * to
last 3 sts, p3.

Next row: *K3, p1, k1, p2, k1, p1* rep from *
to * last 3 sts, k3.

The last 10 rows form the pattern.

Repeat them twice more, ending on a
WS row.

Decrease for Crown

Row 1: *P1, p2tog, KB1, p1, KB1 twice, p1, KB1
* to last 3 sts, p2tog, p1.

Row 2 and all following even rows: Knit all
knit sts and purl all purl sts.

Row 3: P2, *k2, k2tog, k2, p2tog * rep to
last 2 sts, p2.

Row 5: P2, *k2tog, k1, k2tog, p1,* rep to last
2 sts, p2.

Row 7: P2, *sl 1, k2tog, psso, p1 * to last
4 sts, sl 1, k2tog, psso, p2.

Row 9: P1, *k2tog, * rep across row to last
2 sts, p2tog.

Break yarn and run through stitches on
needle, gather up and secure. Sew side
seam neatly. Make a large pompom and
sew securely to the top of the hat.

RIGHT MITTEN

Using US 8 (UK 6 / 5 mm) and yarn, cast
on 30 sts.

Work in k2, p2 rib for 18 rows.

Next row: *K4, p1, kB1, p1, [kB1 twice], p1,
KB1, p1, k4* knit to end.

Next row: Knit all knit stitches and purl all
purl stiches.

**Shape Thumb

Next row: *K4, p1, KB1, k1, [KB1 twice], p1,
KB1, p1, k4*, m1, k1, m1, k13.

Next and all following alt rows: Knit all
knit stitches, purl all purl stitches.

Next row: *K4, p1, CB6k, p1, k4*, m1, k3,
m1, k13.

Next row: *K4, p1, KB1, p1, [KB1 twice], p1,
KB1, p1, k4*, m1, k5, m1, k13.

Next row: *K4, p1, KB1, p1, [KB1 twice], p1,
KB1, p1, k4*, m1, k7, m1, k13 (38 sts).

Next row: Knit all knit stitches and purl all purl stitches.

Work Thumb

Next row: *K4, p1, KB1, p1, [KB1 twice], p1, KB1, p1, k4*, k9 turn, cast on 1 st.

Next row: P10, turn, cast on 1 st (11 sts).

***Work 6 rows in St st on these 11 sts.

Next row: K2tog across row to last st, k1. Break yarn and thread through sts, draw up and fasten off. Sew the thumb seam. With RS facing rejoin yarn to right-hand needle. Pick up and knit 3 sts from the base of the thumb, knit to end of row (31 sts).

Next row: Knit all knit sts and purl all purl sts.

Row 1: *K4, p1, CB6k, p1, k4*, knit to end.

Row 2 and all even rows: Knit all knit sts, purl all purl sts.

Row 3: *K4, p1, KB1, p1 [KB1 twice], p1, KB1, p1, k4 * knit to end.

Row 5: As row 3

Row 7: As row 3

Row 9: As row 1.

Row 10: As row 2.

Keeping continuity of pattern as for last 10 rows for as long as possible, shape top as follows:

Row 1: K1, k2tog, pattern10, k2tog, k1, k2tog, pattern10, k2tog, k1 (27 sts).

Row 2 and all even rows: Knit all knit sts, purl all purl sts.

Row 3: K1, k2tog, pattern8, K2tog, k1, k2tog, pattern8, k2tog, k1 (23 sts).

Row 5: K1, k2tog, pattern6, k2tog, k1, k2tog, pattern6, k2tog, k1 (19 sts).

Row 7: K1, k2tog, pattern4, k2tog, k1, k2tog, pattern4, k2tog, k1 (15 sts).

Row 8: As row 2. Bind off.

Row 5: K13, m1, k5, m1, *k4, p1, KB1, p1, [KB1 twice], p1, KB1, p1, k4.

Row 7: K13, m1, k7, m1, *k4, p1, kB1, p1, [KB1 twice], p1, KB1, p1, k4.

Row 8: As row 2.

Work Thumb

Next row: K22, turn.

Next row: P9, turn.

Complete as Right Mitten from ***

Finishing

Sew side seam and top of mitten.
Fold back cuffs.

LEFT MITTEN

Work as for Right Mitten to **

Shape Thumb

Row 1: K13, m1, k1, m1, *k4, p1, KB1, p1, [KB1 twice], p1, kB1, p1, k4*.

Row 2 and all even rows: Knit all knit sts and purl all purl sts.

Row 3: K13, m1, k3, m1, *k4, p1, CB6k, p1, k4*.

Tunic Top

A sculptured pattern gives this little tunic top a special look. Pair it with leggings or tights for a stylish look or wear it over jeans for a more casual outfit. Knitted in a beautiful soft yarn, which is available in a wide range of colors, it will be hard to decide which one to use.

✳✳✳ Experienced

To fit 2–4 years

MEASUREMENTS

Chest 31 in (71 cm) around chest; length from back neck 19 in (48 cm), adjustable; sleeve seam with cuff turned back 2½ in (6 cm)

MATERIALS

◆ 7 x 50g balls Sirdar Sublime Baby Cashmere / Merino Silk DK, 75% extra fine merino wool / 20% silk / 5% cashmere (50g; 127 yd / 116 m) in ragdoll, shade 0244
◆ Knitting needles size US 3 and 6 (UK 8 and 10 / 3.25 and 4 mm)
◆ 2 stitch holders
◆ 4 flower buttons

GAUGE

22st x 28 rows st st = 4 in (10 cm) square using US 6 (UK 8 / 4 mm)

SLEEVES

With US 3 (UK 10 / 3.25 mm) and main yarn, cast on 55 sts, work 4 in (10 cm) garter stitch.

Change to US 6 (UK 8 / 4 mm). Beg with a knit row, work in St st until piece measures 6 in (15 cm) ending on a purl row.

Shape Armholes

Bind off 5 sts at the beginning of the next 2 rows.

Work 2 rows straight in St st.

Row 5: K2, k2tog, work to last 4 sts, k1, sl 1, psso, k2.

Work 3 rows St st.

Row 9: K2, k2tog, work to last 4 sts, k1, sl 1, psso, k2.

Next row: Purl.

Continue shaping as for rows 9 and 10 until 9 sts remain. Leave sts on a holder. Work second sleeve to match.

BACK

Using US 6 (UK 8 / 4 mm), cast on 99 sts fairly loosely.

Row 1: K1, yo, p5, p3tog, *p5, yo, k1, yo, p5, p3tog*, rep from * to * to last 6 sts, p5, yo, k1.

Row 2 and all even rows: Purl.

Rows 3, 5, 7, 9 and 11: Work as row 1.

Row 13: K1, yo, sl 1, k1, psso, yo, p3, p3tog, *p3, yo, k2tog, yo, k1, yo, sl 1, k1, psso, yo, p3, p3tog* rep from * to * to last 6 sts, p3, yo, k2tog, yo, k1.

Row 15: K1, yo, k1, sl 1, k1, psso, yo, p2, p3tog, *p2, yo, k2tog, k1, yo, k1, yo, sl 1, k1, psso, yo, p2, p3tog* rep from * to * to last 6 sts, p2, yo, k2tog, k1, yo, k1.

Row 17: K1, yo, k2, sl 1, k1, psso, yo, p1, p3tog, *p1, yo, k2tog, k2, yo, k1, yo, k2, sl 1, k1, psso, yo, p1, p3tog* rep from * to * to last 6 sts, p1, yo, k2tog, k2, yo, k1.

Row 19: K1, yo, k3, sl 1, k1, psso, yo, p3tog, *yo, k2tog, k3, yo, k1, yo, k3, sl 1, k1, psso, yo, p3tog* rep from * to * to last 6 sts, yo, k2tog, k3, yo, k1.

Row 21: K4, k2tog, yo, k2 *k1, yo, sl 1, k1, psso, k7, k2tog, yo, k2*, rep from * to * to last 7 sts, k1, yo, k2tog, k4.

Row 23: K3, k2tog, yo, k3, *k2, yo, sl 1, k1, psso, k5, k2tog, yo, k3* rep from * to * to last 7 sts, k2, yo, sl 1, k1, psso, k3.

Row: 25: K2, k2tog, yo, k4, *k3, yo, sl 1, k1, psso, k3, k2tog, yo, k4* rep from * to * to last 7 sts, k3, yo, sl 1, k1, psso, k2.

Row 27: K1, k2tog, yo, k5, *k4, yo, sl 1, k1, psso, k1, k2tog, yo, k5*, rep from * to * to last 7 sts, K4, yo, sl 1, k1, psso, k1.

Row 29: K2tog, yo, k6, *k5, yo, sl 1, k2tog, psso, yo, k6*, rep from * to * to last 7 sts, k5, yo, sl 1, k1, psso.

Row 30: Purl.

Continue in St st, dec 1 st at each end of the next and every following 8th row until there are 83 sts on the needle and work measures approx 12 in (30 cm). Adjust length here if desired.

Shape Armholes

Bind off 5 sts at the beginning of the next two rows.

Next row: K2, k2tog, work to last 4 sts, k1, sl 1, psso, k2.

Next row: Purl.

Continue as for last 2 rows until 31 sts remain. Slip sts onto a holder.

FRONT

Work as back until there are 47 sts.

Shape Neck

Next row: K2, k2tog, k12, turn and work on these sts for first side of neck.

Row 1: P2tog, purl to end.

Row 2: K2, k2tog, work to last 2 sts, k2tog.

Continue as on last 2 rows until 8 sts remain.

Continue to decrease at armhole edge until you have 3 sts.

P3tog and fasten off.

Slip next 15 sts onto a holder for front neck.

Rejoin yarn to remaining sts and work other side of neck as follows:

Next row: K12, skpo, k2.

Complete to match first side, reversing shaping and working skpo instead of k2tog.

Neck Band

With US 3 (UK 10 / 3.25 mm) and RS of work facing, pick up and knit 15 sts down left side of neck, knit across 15 sts on holder, 14 sts up right side of neck, 9 sts from top of sleeve, 31 sts from back neck, and 9 sts from top of other sleeve (93 sts).

Next row: Working in garter stitch, k9, dec 6 sts evenly across k31 sts of back of neck, k44, (87 sts).

Continue in garter stitch for another 8 rows.

Bind off firmly in garter stitch.

Join bound off sts at left front raglan and first 10 rows of raglan shaping.

BUTTONHOLE BAND

With RS facing and using US 3 (UK 10 / 3.25 mm), pick up and knit 37 sts evenly along front raglan edge and neckband.

Work 3 more rows garter stitch.

Buttonhole row: K2, yo, k2tog, *k6, yo, k2tog*, rep from * to last st, k1.

Work 3 more rows garter stitch.

Bind off.

BUTTON BAND

With RS facing and using US 3 (UK 10 / 3.25 mm), pick up and knit 37 sts evenly along back raglan edge. Work another 3 rows garter stitch and bind off.

Finishing

Join side and sleeve seams. Turn cuffs back onto right side of sleeves. Sew on buttons to correspond with button holes.

Fruit and Play Bag

Use bright colored yarn remnants to make these delightful smiley-faced fruit. When it's time to pack the fruit away, store them in their own bag which has been decorated with an apple tree, flowers, and butterflies. Alternatively the bag is perfect for a little girl to take shopping.

❋ **Easy**

Note When finishing the fruit be sure to sew everything very securely if you intend to let very young children play with them.

BAG MEASUREMENTS
10½ in (27 cm) wide x 9 in (22 cm) tall

MATERIALS
Bag:
- Sirdar Baby Aran, Blend: 100% acrylic (100g; 258 yd / 236 m)
- 2 x 100 g balls red poppy, shade 824
- Knitting needles size US 5, 6 and 7 (UK 7, 8 and 9 / 3.75, 4 and 4.5 mm)

- Oddments of green, brown and red DK yarn for the tree
- Flower and butterfly buttons

Fruit:
- Approximately 25 g of DK yarn in: pale yellow, deep yellow, green, black, red-orange, brown and deep purple
- Knitting needles size US 5 (UK 9 / 3.75 mm)
- Safety stuffing
- Black yarn for embroidery

SPECIAL ABBREVIATION
M1 = Make 1 stitch by picking up the strand of yarn that lies between the stitch you are working and the next one on the needle, and working into the back of it.

BAG

Using aran yarn and US 7 (UK 7 / 4.5 mm), cast on 46 sts.

Work in garter stitch for 10 rows.

Row 11: Knit.

Row 12: K8, purl to last 8sts, k8.

Repeat Rows 11 and 12 another 22 times.

Work 6 rows in garter stitch.

*Next row: Knit.

Next row: K8, purl to last 8 sts, k8.

Repeat last 2 rows once more.

Work 4 rows in garter stitch.**

Repeat last 8 rows from * to ** 5 times more, then first 4 rows again.

Work 10 rows garter stitch. Bind off.

HANDLES

Using green DK and US 6 (UK 8 / 4 mm), cast on 60 sts.

Knit 14 rows.

Bind off.

Make 2.

TREE

To make the trunk, using US 5 (UK 9 / 3.75 mm) and brown yarn, cast on 7 sts.

Work in k1, p1 rib for 18 rows. Bind off.

To make foliage, using US 5 (UK 9 / 3.75 mm) and green yarn, cast on 10 sts.

Next row: Inc 1 st at each end.

Next row: Knit.

Repeat last 2 rows until you have 18 sts.

Work 5 rows in St st.

Next row: Dec 1 st at each end.

Next row: Knit.

Repeat last 2 rows until 8 sts remain.

Bind off.

Finishing

Work in all yarn ends neatly. Fold piece in half right sides together and sew side seams. Turn right side out.

Embroider red French knots to depict apples on one side of the foliage at random intervals. Pin foliage and trunk in place on the front St st panel. Sew neatly in place. Sew on flower and butterfly buttons. Pin handles in place on each side of the top of the bag. Sew firmly in place at the base.

PEAR

Using US 5
(UK 9 / 3.75 mm)
and appropriate
color cast on
10 sts.

Knit 1 row.

Row 2: Increase in
each stitch across
row (20 sts).

Row 3: Purl.

Row 4: *K1, inc in next st* across row
(30 sts).

Work 3 rows St st.

Row 8: (K2, increase in next stitch) all
across row (40 sts).

Row 9: Purl.

Work 10 rows in St st.

Row 20: (K2, k2tog) across row.

Work 5 rows in St st beginning with a
purl row.

Row 26: (K1, k2tog) all across row.

Work 5 rows St st beginning with a
purl row.

Row 32: K2tog all across row.

Row 33: Purl.

Don't bind off, but run yarn through
remaining 10 sts and pull up tightly,
fasten off.

ORANGE

Using US 5 (UK 9 /
3.75 mm) and
appropriate color,
cast on 10 sts.

Knit 1 row.

Row 2: Increase in
each stitch across row
(20 sts).

Row 3: Purl.

Row 4: *K1, inc in next st*, all across row
(30 sts).

Work 3 rows St st, beginning with a purl
row.

Row 8: (K2, inc in next stitch) all across
row (40 sts).

Row 9: Purl.

Work 14 rows St st.

Row 24: (K2, k2tog) all across row.

Work 3 rows St st beginning with a
purl row.

Row 28: (K1, k2tog) all across row.

Row 29: Purl.

Row 30: K2tog all across row.

Row 31: Purl.

Don't bind off, but run yarn through remaining 10 sts and pull up tightly, fasten off.

PLUM

Using US 5 (UK 9 / 3.75 mm) and appropriate color, cast on 5 sts.

Row 1: Purl.

Row 2: Inc in each st to end of row (10 sts).

Row 3: Purl.

Row 4: Increase in each stitch across row (20 sts).

Row 5: Purl.

Work 4 rows St st.

Row 10: (K2, k2tog), to end.

Row 11: Purl.

Row 12: (K1, k2tog), to end.

Row 13: Purl.

Row 14: K2tog across row.

Row 15: P2tog across row to last st, p1.

Row 16: K3tog, fasten off.

APPLE

Using US 5 (UK 9 / 3.75 mm) and appropriate color, cast on 10 sts.

Knit 1 row.

Row 2: Increase in each stitch across row (20 sts).

Row 3: Purl.

Row 4: (K1, inc in next st) all across row (30 sts).

Work 3 rows St st.

Row 8: (K2, inc in next stitch) all across row (40 sts).

Row 9: Purl.

Work 10 rows St st on these stitches.

Row 20: (K2, k2tog) all across row.

Work 3 rows St st beginning with a purl row.

Row 24: (K1, k2tog) all across row.

Row 25: Purl.

Row 26: K2tog all across row.

Row 27: Purl.

Don't bind off, but run yarn through remaining 10 sts and pull up tightly, fasten off.

LEMON

Using US 5 (UK 9 / 3.75 mm) and yellow yarn, cast on 5 sts.

Row 1: Purl.

Row 2: Inc in each st to end of row (10 sts).

Row 3: Purl.

Row 4: Inc in each stitch across row (20 sts).

Row 5: Purl.

Row 6: (K1, inc in next st), all across row (30 sts).

Row 7: Purl.

Work 4 rows St st.

Row 8: (K3, k2tog) to end.

Work 3 rows St st.

Row 12: (K2, k2tog) to end.

Row 13: Purl.

Row 14: (K1, k2tog) to end.

Row 15: Purl.

Row 16: K2tog across row.

Row 17: P2tog across row.

Row 18: K3tog, fasten off.

BANANA

Using US 5 (UK 9 / 3.75 mm) and black yarn, cast on 8 sts.

Knit 2 rows garter stitch.

Break off black yarn and join in pale green.

Work 2 rows St st.

Break green yarn and join in yellow yarn.

Inc 1 st at each end of the next and every alt row until you have 14 sts.

Row 6: Purl.

Row 7: Inc in first st, k6, m1 work to last stitch, inc 1.

Work 3 rows St st beginning with a purl row.

Row 11: Inc in first st, k7, m1, k8, inc in last st (20 sts).

Work 3 rows St st beginning with a purl row.

Row 15: Inc in first st, k9, m1, k9, inc in last st (23 sts).

Row 16: Purl.

Row 17: Inc in first st, k10, m1, k11, inc in last st (26 sts).

Row 18: Purl.

Row 19: Inc in first st, k12, m1, k12, inc in last st (29 sts).

Row 20: Purl.

Work 6 rows straight in St st.

Row 27: K14, turn and purl to end.

Row 28: K15, turn and purl to end.

Row 29: K16, turn and purl to end.

Row 30: K17, turn and purl to end.

Work in St st for 6 rows ending on a purl row.

Row 37: Dec 1 st at each end of next row.

Row 38: Purl.

Row 39: K2tog, k10, k2tog, work to last 2 sts, k2tog.

Work 3 rows St st beginning with a purl row.

Row 43: K2tog, k9, k2tog, work to last 2 sts, k2tog.

Row 44: Purl.

Dec 1 st at each end of next and following alternate rows until 9 sts remain.

Work 5 rows straight in St st. Bind off.

STALKS

Using US 5 (UK 9 / 3.75 mm) and brown yarn, cast on 6 sts.

Knit 2 rows garter stitch. Bind off.

LEAVES

Using US 5 (UK 9 / 3.75 mm) and green, cast on 5 sts.

Knit 2 rows garter stitch.

Row 3: K2, m1, k1, m1, k2 (7 sts).

Row 4: K3, p1, k3.

Row 5: K3, m1, k1, m1, k3. (9 sts).

Row 6: K4, p1, k4.

Row 7: Knit.

Repeat last 2 rows twice more.

Dec 1 st at each end of next and every following row until 3 sts remain.

Next row: K3tog, fasten off.

Finishing

Apple

Sew side seam of apple, stuff firmly, shape and close seam. Sew a stalk and a leaf securely to the top of the apple.

Orange

Sew and stuff as for the apple but use the reverse side of the knitting to give the textured effect of the rind. Embroider a French knot on the top and bottom of the fruit using black yarn.

Pear

Sew and stuff as for the apple, remembering that the pear will be "fatter" at the bottom and taper toward the top. Attach leaves to top of pear.

Lemon:

Sew up, stuff and shape as for the apple.

Plum

Sew up, stuff and shape as for the apple. Attach a stalk and leaf.

Banana

Sew the side seam of the banana. Stuff firmly. Bend the fruit a little in the center to give a curved shape. Thread a needle with yellow yarn and work three rows of chain stitch along the length of the banana to give definition to the skin. Use black yarn to embroider happy faces onto the fruit.

Striped Socks

A beautifully soft cashmere-wool mixed yarn is used to make these little socks. Three balls of yarn are used at the same time for the shaping, which makes the pattern a little tricky. It is simple to add length in the leg and also in the foot to create bigger sizes.

❉❉ Intermediate

To fit 3–5 years; foot and leg length is adjustable

Tip The socks can be made just using one shade of yarn if desired

GAUGE

24 sts x 32 rows st st = 4 in (10 cm) square using US 5 (UK 9 / 3.75 mm) knitting needles

MATERIALS

- Rowan Cashsoft DK, 57% extrafine merino/10% cashmere/33% acrylic microfiber (50g; 126 yd / 115 m)
- 1 x 50g ball in poppy, shade 512 (A)
- 1 x 50g ball blue jacket, shade 535 (B)
- Knitting needles size US 5 (UK 9 / 3.75 mm)

Stripe pattern is knitted by alternating 2 rows A with 2 rows B st st.

Make 2.

Using size US 5 (UK 9 / 3.75 mm) and **A**, cast on 43 sts.

Row 1: K1, p1 , rep to last st, k1.

Row 2: P1, k1, rep to last st, p1.

Work in k1, p1 rib for 2 rows.

Change to B and work another 14 rows in rib.

Change to St st and work *2 rows B, 2 rows A*, rep from * to * twice more, then work 2 rows B. (Adjust length of leg at this point, if desired).

Shape Heel

Using poppy, k12, turn, work in St st for another 15 rows, ending with a purl row, turn.

Next row: K3, k2tog, k1, turn, sl 1, p4, turn.

Next row: K4, k2tog, k1, turn, sl 1, p5, turn.

Next row: K5, k2tog, k1, turn, sl 1, p6, turn.

Next row: K6, k2tog, k1 (8 sts).

Next row: Purl.

Using A, k8, pick up and k10 sts along side

of heel, knit to end of row.

Next row: P12, turn and work on these sts for second side of heel.

Work 15 rows St st ending with a knit row. Work other side of heel as follows:

Next row: P3, p2tog, p1, turn, sl 1, k4, turn.

Next row: P4, p2tog, p1, turn, sl 1, k5, turn.

Next row: P5, p2tog, p1, turn, sl 1, k6, turn.

Next row: Knit.

Next row: P6, p2tog, p1 (8 sts).

Now pick up and purl 10 sts along side of heel, purl to end of row.

Note To maintain the striped pattern over the instep you will need to join in a separate ball of A at each end of the row and join in B as required.

Continue heel shaping as follows:

Next row: K16, k2tog, k19B, k2tog tbl, k16.

Next row: P17A, k19B, k17A.

Next row: K15, k2tog, k19A, sl 1, k1, k2tog tbl, k15.

Next row: Purl using A.

Next row: K14, k2tog, k19B, K2tog tbl, k14.

Next row: P15A, 19B, 15A.

Next row: Using A k13, k2tog, k19, K2tog tbl, k13.

Next row: Purl using A.

Next row: K12, k2tog, k19B, k2togtbl, k12.

Next row: P13A, p19B, p13A.

Next row: Using A k11, k2tog, k19, K2tog tbl, k11.

Next row: Using A purl across all sts (43 sts).

Continue on these sts, working 2 rows B, 2 rows A until work measures desired length, ending on a purl row of a B stripe.

Shape Toe

Next row: Using A only for toe, k9, k2tog, k2, k2tog tbl, k13, k2tog, k2, k2tog tbl, k9.

Next row: Purl.

Next row: K8, k2tog, k2, k2tog tbl, k11, k2tog, k2, k2tog tbl, k8.

Next row: Purl.

Next row: K7, k2tog, k2, k2tog tbl, k9, k2tog, k2, k2tog tbl, k7.

Continue decreasing 4 sts on every alt row, until 19 sts remain ending on a purl row. Bind off.

Finishing

Sew in all ends neatly. Sew foot and back seam using a flat seam. Turn cuff back on top of sock, if required.

Shawl-neck Sweater

Wide stockinette stitch stripes and a shawl collar make this a perfect rough and tumble sweater. It will keep a little person warm and snug when going to the park or when playing in the yard. Aran-weight yarn makes the sweater quick to knit and has a wide range of colors available. You could also make it a solid color if you like.

✳✳ **Intermediate**

To fit 1–2 years (2–3 years/3–4 years)

GAUGE

18 sts x 24 rows st st = 4 in (10 cm) square using US 7 (UK 7 / 4.5 mm) knitting needles

MEASUREMENTS

Chest 20–22 (22–24, 24–26) in,
51–56 (56–61, 61–66) cm;
length from back neck 12 (13½, 16) in,
30 (34, 40) cm;
sleeve length 7 (8 9½) in, 17 (20, 24) cm

MATERIALS

◆ Sirdar Supersoft Aran weight 100% supersoft acrylic (100g; 258yd / 236 m)
◆ 2 (2, 3) x 100 g balls river blue, shade 877 (A)
◆ 1 (1, 2) x 100 g ball cream, shade 831 (B)
◆ Knitting needles sizes US 6 and 7 (UK 7 and 8 / 4 and 4.5 mm)
◆ Stitch holder

Note Carry yarn not in use loosely up side of work.

BACK

Using US 6 (UK 8 / 4 mm) and A, cast on 50 (56, 60) sts.

Work in k2, p2 rib for 2½ in (6 cm) for all sizes.

Change to US 7 (UK 7 / 4.5 mm). Join in yarn B and change to St st, working in stripes of 6 rows yarn A and 6 rows yarn B. Continue until back measures 11 (12½, 15 in) or 28 (32, 38) cm ending with a purl row.

Shape Shoulders

Bind off 8 (9, 9) sts at beg of next 2 rows, and 8 (9, 10) sts at beg of following 2 rows. Bind off remaining 18 (20, 22) sts.

FRONT

Work as for back until front measures 7½ (9, 10½ in) or 19 (23, 27) cm ending with a purl row.

Keeping continuity of stripe pattern,

Shape Neck as follows

Next row: K16 (18, 19) turn and work on this side first, leaving remaining sts on a holder.

Continue until work measures 11 (12½,

15) in or 28 (32, 38) cm ending on a purl row.

Shape Shoulder

Next row: Bind off 8 (9, 9) sts, work to end.

Next row: Purl.

Next row: Bind off remaining stitches.

Return to stitches on holder and rejoin appropriate color.

Bind off 18 (20, 22) sts for center neck, knit to end.

Complete to match first half, reversing shoulder shapings.

SLEEVES

Using thumb method, US 6 (UK 8 / 4 mm) and A, cast on 35 (35, 37) sts

Work in k2, p2 rib for 2 in (5 cm) for all sizes.

Change to US 7 (UK 7 / 4.5 mm) knitting needles.

Join in B and work in stripe pattern as for back, AT THE SAME TIME inc 1 st at each end of the 5th and every following 14th (6th, 8th) row until there are 39 (45, 49) sts. Continue without shaping until sleeve

measures 7 (8, 9½) in or 17 (20, 24) cm
ending on a purl row.

Shape Top of Sleeve
Bind off 3 (4, 3) sts at beg of next 2 (4, 8)
rows.
Bind off 4 (5, 4) sts at beg of next 6 (4, 4)
rows.
Bind off remaining stitches.
Make 2.

SHAWL COLLAR
Using US 6 (UK 8 / 4 mm) and A, cast on
116 (116, 124) sts.
Row 1: P1, k2, (p2, k2 to last st), p1.
Row 2: K1 (p2, k2 to last 3 sts), p2, k1.
Rows 1 and 2 set the rib pattern. Continue
in rib until collar measures 3½ (4, 4½ in)
or 9 (10, 12) cm ending on a row 2. Bind
off loosely in rib.

Finishing
Sew in all yarn ends. Press all
pieces following yarn manufacturer's
instructions. Join front and back shoulder
seams with RS together. Fold sleeve in
half lengthways, RS together and mark

center point. Match center of sleeve to
shoulder seam, sew sleeves in position.
Join side and sleeve seams.
Placing left over right, sew side edges
of collar to bind-off stitches on center
front of neck. Sew bind-off edge of collar
evenly in place all around neck edge.

Angora Hat and Fingerless Gloves

This pretty hat complete with a flower and leaf detail is a perfect match with a pair of fingerless gloves. The yarn used is a luxurious angora and lambswool mix and is soft and warm to the touch. Just one ball is all that you will need to make both projects.

✳✳ Intermediate

MEASUREMENTS
To fit 3–5 years
Beanie: Width 17–18 in (46 cm);
depth 7 in (18 cm)
Gloves: Length 5½ in (12 cm); width around
palm 6 in (15 cm)

GAUGE
24st x 26 rows st st = 4 in (10 cm) square
worked over St st US 6 (UK 8 / 4 mm)

MATERIALS
◆ 1 x 50 g ball Orkney 50% angora/
  50% lambswool (50g; 218 yd/ 199 m) in
  Periodot (will knit up the hat and gloves)
◆ Knitting needles size US 5 and 6
  (UK 8 and 9 / 3.75 and 4 mm)

SPECIAL ABBREVIATIONS
Skpo = Sl1, k1, pass slipped stitch over, to
decreae a stitch.

Tip This yarn sheds a little to begin with
so knit with a cloth over your knees.

Using US 6 (UK 8 / 4 mm), cast on 90 sts.
Knit 1 row.

Row 2: (RS) K1,*k2tog twice, [yo, k1]
3 times, yo, [skpo] twice, rep from
* to last st, k1.

Row 3: Purl

Rows 4 and 5: Knit

These last 4 rows form the pattern and
are repeated. Work last 4 rows 8 more
times.

Work 2 rows in St st.

Continue in St st and shape crown:

Row 1: *K5, k2tog* to last 6 sts, k6
(78 sts).

Rows 2-4: St st.

Row 5: *K4, k2tog* to last 6 sts, k6
(66 sts)

Rows 6-8: St st.

Row 9: *K3, k2tog* to last st, k1 (53 sts).

Rows 10-12: St st.

Row 13: *K2, k2tog* to last st, k1 (40 sts).

Rows 14-16: St st.

Row 17: *K1, k2tog* to last st, k1 (27 sts).

Row 18: Purl.

Row 19: K2tog across row to last st, k1
(14 sts).

Break yarn, thread through stitches on
needle, draw up and fasten off.

FLOWERS

Using US 5 (UK 9 / 3.75 mm), cast on
14 sts.

Row 1: Purl.

Row 2: Inc in every stitch to end of row.

Row 3: Knit.

Row 4: Bind off 2 sts, *yo and slip stitch
on needle over the yo, k1, bind off 1*, rep
from * to *. Continue binding off in this
manner until all stitches are worked.
Fasten off. The piece will curl as you bind
off. Form the curl into a rose. Secure with
a few stitches.
Make 2.

LEAVES

Using US 5 (UK 9 / 3.75 mm), cast on
10 sts.
Knit 2 rows.

Row 3: Bind off 6 sts, knit to end.

Row 4: **K4, cast on 6 sts.

Row 5: Knit.

Row 6: Knit.**

Row 7: Bind off 6 sts, knit to end.
Rep from ** to ** and bind off all stitches.

Finishing

Sew side seam of hat. Seam will run down the back of the head. Attach flowers and leaves to one side of the hat

GLOVES

Using US 6 (UK 8 / 4 mm), cast on 35 sts. Knit 1 row.
Row 2: (RS) K1, *k2tog twice, [yo, k1,] 3 times, yo, [skpo] twice , rep from * to last st, k1.
Row 3: Purl
Row 4 and 5: Knit
Rows 2–5 form the pattern. Repeat the pattern twice more.
Work 18 rows St st.
Change to US 5 (UK 9 / 3.75 mm).
Work 7 rows garter st. Bind off.
Make two flowers as for hat, but cast on 8 sts instead of 14. Make 2

Finishing

Sew in ends. Fold glove in half and sew side seam, leaving an opening for thumb. Attach a flower to the back of each glove.

About the Author

Knitting and crochet have been a lifelong passion
for Val Pierce. She was taught to knit when she
was just 5 years old and progressed from making
dolls clothes and scarves to knitting garments for
friends and family. Later she was a pattern checker
for knitwear designers and yarn companies, before
becoming a designer herself. Val began designing
regularly for several magazines and had her first
book, *Cutest Ever Baby Knits*, published in 2010
by Trafalgar Square Books. Since then she has
written many more knitting and crochet books. Val
particularly loves designing for children and babies.
She lives and works in Shropshire in the UK.

Index